Wit

ALSO BY JOHN TRAIN

Literary criticism

Wit

The Best Things Ever Said

by
. . . Mark Twain, Oscar Wilde, Disraeli,
Voltaire, Dorothy Parker, Winston Churchill,
Talleyrand, P. G. Wodehouse,
George Bernard Shaw . . .

Compiled and Edited by

John Train

Illustrated by Pierre Le-Tan

Edward Burlingame Books
An Imprint of HarperCollins*Publishers*

FIRST EDITION

Designed by Katy Homans

Typeset in Monotype Dante by Michael & Winifred Bixler

Library of Congress Cataloging-in-Publication Data

Wit/[compiled and edited by] John Train.—1st ed.

p.   cm.

Includes index.

ISBN 0-06-018223-7 (cloth)

1. Anecdotes.   I. Train, John.

PN6261.W57   1991

082—dc20

91–55510

91 92 93 94 95   CW   10 9 8 7 6 5 4 3

CONTENTS

To
Linda Kelly,
my collaborator,
with love

PREFACE

Wit, said Alexander Pope, is "What oft was thought, but ne'er so well expressed." Auden complained that La Rochefoucauld only told us what we had always known; I like Robert Craft's response that without him some of us would not have known that we knew. In other words, the essence of wit is verbal felicity, unlike humor, which is based on character and situations. Will Rogers and Mark Twain are usually humorous rather than witty, while Bernard Shaw and F. E. Smith are witty rather than humorous. Wit surprises, humor illuminates; wit is often aristocratic in its clever superiority, while humor is usually popular.*

*Fowler's admirable table is too good not to cite:

	Motive or Aim	Province	Method or Means	Audience
humor	discovery	human nature	observation	the sympathetic
wit	throwing light	words, ideas	surprise	the intelligent
satire	amendment	morals, manners	accentuation	the self-satisfied
sarcasm	inflicting pain	faults, foibles	inversion	victim, bystander
invective	discredit	misconduct	direct statement	the public
irony	exclusiveness	statement of facts	mystification	an inner circle
cynicism	self-justification	morals	exposure of nakedness	the respectable
the sardonic	self-relief	adversity	pessimism	self

Source: H. W. Fowler, A Dictionary of Modern English Usage (London: Oxford University Press/Humphrey Milford, 1940).

England seems fonder of wit than America. One reason is the oratorical style of Parliament, the most widely noted forum in the land. MPs do not have fixed desks, so they gather in the front rows of the chamber, facing each other a few yards apart. This invites the robust cut and thrust of Parliamentary exchanges, where wit is a powerful weapon, since the House is as glad to be entertained as instructed. Thus, the great Edmund Burke was called, at the time, "the dinner bell," while Disraeli and other great Parliamentary debaters made a point of being witty. Dizzy, announcing a series of Church of England preferments, was once caught out by an opposition member who asked what the duties of an archdeacon actually were. Having no idea, he solemnly intoned, "The duties of an archdeacon consist in the prompt and efficient discharge of his archidiaconal functions." The House, far from hooting, was delighted.

In Congress a speaker holds forth to a near-empty chamber—the members present being scattered about at their individual desks—and then asks permission to "revise and extend" his pronouncements for publication in the *Congressional Record*, perhaps to be mailed to his constituents. So he is really addressing an absent audience. In America, as Adlai Stevenson—himself a very witty man—complained, the electorate assumes that a clever politician must be unsound, and a ponderous one worth listening to. So perhaps that is why many witticisms have English (and aristocratic) origins.

A category of verbal felicity not considered by Fowler is lapidary prose, an idea expressed so perfectly that you know it could never be done better. It is wit that is not necessarily amusing. Consider the motto of the U.S. Panama Canal Company: THE LAND DIVIDED, THE WORLD UNITED. Or this tribute to Benjamin Franklin: ERIPUIT COELO FULMEN, SCEPTRUMQUE TYRANNIS: "From the sky he snatched lightning, and from the tyrant, his scepter." Wonderful!* I offer a few examples of the genre in this little collection. I've also thrown in, just because I like them, some humorous odds and ends that may not fit the definition of wit at all: on occasion one must be prepared to rise above principle.

As for the French, to my mind their concept of wit—*esprit*—means brilliant juggling with ideas. Their language is rich in concepts that other tongues do not

---

Claimed by both Turgot and von der Trenck. Franklin's epitaph for himself is much beloved:

> The body of B. Franklin, printer,
> Like the cover of an old book,
> Its contents torn out,
> And stript of its lettering and gilding
> Lies here, food for worms.
> But the work itself shall not be lost;
> For it will, as he believed, appear once more
> In a new and more elegant edition,
> Corrected and amended
> By its author.

even identify, some even referring to wit itself. For instance, *l'esprit d'escalier*, "wit of the staircase": when you think of a marvelous retort some minutes too late, on the way downstairs. The literary variation is when great ideas come to you after the book is at the printer's. I will doubtless think of splendid things to add to this preface . . . too late!

I am most grateful to Sara Perkins for editorial assistance, and to Elena Bonham-Carter for suggestions.

Wit

LOVE

A Trois

The chain of marriage is so heavy that it takes two to bear it; sometimes three.   —Alexandre Dumas *fils*

Help Wanted

The man who marries his mistress creates a vacancy in the position.   —Jimmy Goldsmith

Anatomy

As a young man I used to have four supple members and one stiff one. Now I have four stiff and one supple.
     —Henri, duc d'Aumale

Profusion

The Prince of Wales (later King Edward VII) said testily to his mistress, Lillie Langtry, "I've spent enough on you to buy a battleship!"

Her answer was, "And you've spent enough *in* me to float one."

Access

Outside every thin woman is a fat man trying to get in.*   —Katherine Whitehorn

Relief

Much-admired actress Mrs. Patrick Campbell called marriage "the deep, deep peace of the double bed after the hurly-burly of the chaise longue."

* *Referring of course to Cyril Connolly's remark that inside every fat man is a thin one wildly signaling to get out. Connolly also observed, "Love is a besieger with friends in the garrison," a gloss on Marguerite de Valois' "In love, as in war, a fortress that negotiates is half taken."*

LAW

Job Description

Edward Corson was cross-examining. "Do you drink?" he asked, looking keenly at the witness.

"That's my business," was the reply.

"And do you have any *other* business?" countered Corson.

Passing Concern

At his execution, Thomas More found the scaffold rickety: unsafe, one might say. Addressing the officer in charge, he said, "I pray thee see me up safe, and for my coming down let me shift for myself."

—Cayley, *Memoirs of More*

Judicial Restraint

As a young lawyer, F. E. Smith (later Lord Birkenhead) was retained by a tram company that had been sued for damages by an injured boy. He appeared before a Judge Willis, who was given to sententious pronouncements. "Poor boy, poor boy," said the judge. "Blind. Put him in that chair so the jury can see him."

SMITH (*sardonically*): Perhaps Your Honor would like to have the boy passed round the jury box.

JUDGE WILLIS (*glaring*): That is a most improper remark!

SMITH: It was provoked by a most improper suggestion.

JUDGE WILLIS (*pausing to gain control of his temper*): Mr. Smith, have you ever heard of a saying by Bacon— the great Bacon—that youth and discretion are ill-wed companions?

SMITH: Indeed I have, Your Honor; and has Your Honor ever heard of a saying by Bacon—the great Bacon— that a much-talking judge is like an ill-tuned cymbal?

JUDGE WILLIS (*livid with fury*): You are extremely offensive, young man!

SMITH: As a matter of fact we both are. The only difference between us is that I am trying to be and you can't help it. I have been listened to with respect by the highest tribunal in the land and I have not come down here to be browbeaten!

On another occasion, Judge Willis demanded: "What do you suppose I am on the bench *for*, Mr. Smith?"

"It is not for me, your Honor," replied F. E., "to attempt to fathom the inscrutable workings of Providence."

Felonious Tool

Jack London, reporting from Japan before World War II, strayed into a restricted zone. The police arrested him and confiscated his camera. On the assurance of the U.S. mission that his intentions were innocent he was released—but without the camera, since the foreign ministry insisted that the instrument of an offense invariably became government property. Lloyd Griscom describes the sequel:

I turned to the Foreign Minister. "If I can name a crime to which this does not apply, will you release the camera?"

Regarding me doubtfully for a few seconds, Baron Komura replied, "Yes, I will."

"Well, what about rape?"

. . . Later the Foreign Minister called me on the telephone. "Mr. Griscom, your story broke up the Cabinet meeting. Mr. London gets his camera back."

Professional Courtesy

A local lawyer opposing New York City attorney Rufus Choate in the White Plains County Court urged the jury to disregard his "Chesterfieldian urbanity."

Choate blandly replied that this might be preferable to the other advocate's "Westchesterfieldian suburbanity."*

* *His kinsman, Joseph Choate, American ambassador in London, was leaving a reception when the Argentine ambassador told him, "Call me a cab!" "You're a cab, sir," answered Choate.*

THE THEATER

Candor

A reporter conducting a tedious interview with musical-comedy librettist Abe Burrows finally inquired, "Mr. Burrows, what was the low point of your life?"

"I hate to say so, kid," Burrows replied, "but I think this is it."

Applause

Shaw's *Candida* opened in New York with Cornelia Otis Skinner in the title role. The critics were enraptured, and Shaw cabled the actress: EXCELLENT. GREATEST. G. B. S.

Miss Skinner replied: UNDESERVING SUCH PRAISE.

Shaw cabled: I MEANT THE PLAY.

To which she answered: SO DID I.

Pacifier

Appearing in a play entitled *Redemption*, John Barrymore was infuriated by the audience's coughing. When the noise resumed during the next act, Barrymore tugged a huge fish from inside his clothes and hurled it across the footlights. "Chew on that, you walruses," he bayed, "while the rest of us get on with the libretto!"

Tiens, C'est Elle

When Sarah Bernhardt, France's greatest actress, had to have a leg amputated, speculation ran high on how she would play her roles when she returned to the stage: reclining? standing? immobile?

Sacha Guitry was in the theater for this long-awaited moment. The house lights dimmed. From behind the curtain, the *régisseur* gave the ritual three knocks on the floor with his staff.

Guitry clutched his companion's elbow. "Aha!" he hissed . . . "That's her!"

Max Beerbohm on Eleonora Duse's Acting

Age cannot wither her nor custom stale her endless uniformity.

Tiens, c'est elle

Role Model

Sarah Bernhardt was playing Cleopatra in London. She screamed, raved, foamed at the mouth, tore her clothing, ripped the curtains from the wall, smashed the furniture. Finally, of course, she killed herself.

A middle-aged lady in the audience said complacently to her companion, "How different, how *very* different, from the home life of our own dear queen!"

Eugenics

The beauteous Mrs. Pat Campbell sighed to Bernard Shaw, "What a wonderful child we would have, with my looks and your brains."

"But suppose," mused Shaw, "it had *my* looks and *your* brains!"

More Shaviana

Rummaging in a secondhand book store, GBS unearthed one of his own works inscribed to a friend, "Compliments of George Bernard Shaw." He bought the book and sent it to the same friend, further inscribed, "With the renewed compliments of George Bernard Shaw."

Once, when a heckler booed him, Shaw stepped to the edge of the stage, peered up at the balcony, and said, "My dear sir, I quite agree with you. But who are we among so many?"

DINING OUT

*Outback Breakfast**

"A piss and a look around."

Box About

Sir Walter Raleigh, being invited to dinner with some great person, where his son was to goe with him: He sayd to his Son, Thou art such a quarrelsome, affronting creature that I am ashamed to have such a Beare in my Company. Mr. Walt humbled himselfe to his father, and promised he would behave himselfe mightily mannerly. So away they went, and Sir Benjamin, I thinke, with them. He sate next to his Father and was very demure at leaste halfe dinner time. Then sayd he, I this morning, not having the feare of God before my eies, but by the instigation of the devill, went to a Whore. I was very eager of her, kissed and embrased her, and went to enjoy her, but she thrust me from her, and vowed I should not, For your father lay with me but an hower ago. Sir Walt, being so

* *Aussie jest.*

strangely supprized and putt out of his countenance at so great a Table, gives his son a damned blow over the face; his son, as rude as he was, would not strike his father, but strikes over the face of the Gentleman that sate next to him, and sayed, Box about, 'twill come to my Father anon.　　　　　—John Aubrey, *Brief Lives*

Refinement

At a dinner where tongue was the main course the lady sitting next to F. E. Smith exclaimed how disgusting it was to eat something that had been in an animal's mouth.

"Have an egg," said Smith.*

Alternatives

Lord Sandwich had dined one day in Foote's (Samuel Foote, the playwright, 1720–77) company, in Covent Garden at the famous Beef Steak Club. The glass had gone profusely round: and at the unguarded time when the bold idea of the moment sallies forth without any regard to good manners:

---

* *To a breakfast guest Tennyson once said, "Have a hegg." After a while he added, anxiously, "You realize, I trust, that I was joking."*

"Foote," said Lord Sandwich, "I have often wondered what catastrophe would bring *you* to your end; but I think you must either die of the pox, or the halter."*

"My Lord," replied Foote instantaneously, "that will depend upon one of two contingencies—whether I embrace your Lordship's mistress or your Lordship's principles."

—*Memoirs of The Life and Writings of Percival Stockdale, Written by Himself*, 1809

The Butler's Humor

Mrs. Ronnie Greville, a celebrated London hostess of the 1930s, kept a notepad by her side at table to record observations on the food, wine, flowers, and service. At a very grand luncheon for the foreign secretary, Austen Chamberlain, she noticed with horror that the butler was intoxicated. She scribbled a note and handed it to him: "You are disgustingly drunk. Leave the room at once." The butler glanced at the note, bowed, folded it, placed it on a silver salver, and carried it around to Chamberlain.

"Ah, from the Foreign Office, no doubt," said Chamberlain portentously.

---

* *On the gallows.*

Fare of State

While at Frederick the Great's court, Voltaire was late for a state dinner. Frederick wrote a note and put it under Voltaire's plate. It said:

> *Voltaire ist ein Esel.**
> Frederick II

Voltaire came to the table, apologizing for being late. As he started to eat Frederick stopped him and told him to read the note under his plate. Voltaire read the note and apologized again. Frederick insisted that he stand up before the whole party and read the note aloud, which he did, in German, but emphasizing the words as follows:

> Voltaire is *one* ass.
> Frederick the *second.*

Changing the Subject

At a dinner party, Oscar Wilde bet that he could produce a witticism about any subject that was offered.

"Queen Victoria," suggested another guest.

"Ah," said Wilde, "but she is not a subject."

---

* *"Voltaire is an [or "one"] ass."* Frederick once invited Voltaire to dinner at Sans Souci thus: "$\frac{P}{A} \frac{c}{100}$" ("Grand souper à Sans Souci" —*that is,* "Grand—sous p—A, cent sous c"). *Voltaire replied* "G a" ("J'ai grand appetit"—*that is,* G grand, a petit).

Social Comments

At a bibulous soirée, Dorothy Parker purred, "One more drink and I'll be under the host."

Of a woman, she wrote, "She wore a low but futile décolletage."

Contemplating the girls at a Yale football weekend, she observed, "If all those sweet young things were laid end to end, I wouldn't be a bit surprised."

Resignation

What would life be without coffee? But then, what is it even with coffee? —Louis XV

Direction

At a lunch party in the country, the company was startled by the sight of two dogs copulating on the lawn.

"What are they doing?" a child inquired.

Noël Coward spoke soothingly: "You see, my dear, the dog in front is blind, and the one behind is pushing him where they have to go."

POLITICS

Summation

Clarence Darrow's eulogy on President Calvin Coolidge: "The greatest man who ever came out of Plymouth Corner, Vermont."

Take Your Time

A government advertisement in the Paris Métro when Mendès-France was trying to wean the French from alcohol to milk: *"L'alcool tue lentement."**

"Tant mieux. Nous ne sommes pas pressés,"† wrote a wag beneath.

Tolerance

Robert Frost defined a liberal as "a man too broadminded to take his own side in a quarrel."

---

* *"Alcohol kills slowly."*

† *"Fine. We're not in a hurry."*

Mismatch

Sir Alec Douglas-Home was asked what would have happened if Khrushchev had been assassinated instead of Kennedy. "I doubt that Aristotle Onassis would have married Mrs. Khrushchev," he replied.

Modest Demeanor

Winston Churchill on Clement Attlee: "A sheep in sheep's clothing."

Heil

Oswald Mosley, the British neofascist leader, was addressing a political rally. As he raised his arm in the Nazi salute a voice from the back called, "All right, Oswald, you may be excused!"

Political Development

F. E. Smith on Bolshevism: "Nature has no cure for this sort of madness, though I have known a legacy from a rich relative to work wonders."

Prediction

"The Soviet Union would remain a one-party nation even if an opposition party were permitted," said Ronald Reagan, "because everyone would join that party."

Inherited Looks

Talleyrand was annoyed by a young man who went on and on about how beautiful his mother was. Finally he inquired, "So your *father* was the ugly one?"*

* *"C'est donc monsieur votre père qui n'était pas beau?"*

RELIGION

Délice

A Frenchwoman, on first tasting chocolate: "Delicious! What a pity it's not a sin!"

The Auld Kirk

SCOTTISH PREACHER (haranguing his flock): At the day of judgment there will be wailing and gnashing of teeth!

VOICE FROM CONGREGATION: What about people who've lost their teeth?

PREACHER (grimly): Teeth will be *provided*!

Theology

In an examination at Oxford, Oscar Wilde was required to translate at sight from the Greek version of the New Testament. The passage chosen was from the story of the Passion. Wilde began to translate, easily and accurately. The examiners were impressed and told him to stop: It was enough. Ignoring them, Wilde continued. At last the examiners were able to halt him; they were quite satisfied. "Oh, do let me go on," said Wilde. "I want to see how it ends."

How Odd of God

The British scientist J. B. S. Haldane was asked what his studies had revealed to him about the nature of God. "An inordinate fondness for beetles," Haldane replied.

Noblesse Oblige

The Queen (Victoria) was at Osborne, and she went out for her customary drive with Lady Errol, who was then in waiting. These dear, elderly ladies, swathed in crepe, drove in an open carriage called a sociable. The Queen was silent and Loelia (Lady Errol) thought it time to make a little conversation. She said, "Oh, your Majesty, think of when we shall see our dear ones again in heaven."

"Yes," said the Queen.

"We shall all meet in Abraham's bosom," said Loelia.

"I will *not* meet Abraham," said the Queen.

—Princess Marie Louise, *Memories of Six Reigns*

Good Works

It is said of American missionaries in Hawaii, whose descendants prospered and then took the islands over, that "they came to do good, and did well."

The Africans say, "Once we had the land and the white man had the Bible. Then, we had the Bible and the white man had the land."

Tact

Exhorted on his deathbed at least to repudiate the devil, unbeliever Voltaire replied, "Is this a time to be making enemies?"

ARTS AND LETTERS

Mark Twain

. . . On a book by Henry James
Once you've put it down, you simply can't pick it up!

. . . and on his father's progress
When I was a boy of fourteen, my father was so igno-
rant I could hardly stand to have him around. But
when I got to be twenty-one, I was astonished at how
much he had learned in seven years.

Transformation

Madame de Staël's novel *Delphine* contains a portrait
of her former lover Talleyrand in the guise of the
charming but treacherous Madame Vernon, while she
herself (whose features in fact had a distinctly mas-
culine cast) appears as the beauteous and feminine
Delphine.

Talleyrand had his revenge: "I hear," he remarked
to Madame de Staël, "that you've written a book in
which both you and I are disguised as women."

Literary Judgment

A young author, sending samples of her work to Somerset Maugham, asked if she should put more *fire* in her stories.

"No—vice versa," answered Maugham.

Homily

When Matthew Arnold carried off Thomas Henry Huxley's umbrella, the great biologist wrote the poet this letter:

My dear Arnold:
Look at Bishop Wilson on the sin of covetousness and then inspect your umbrella stand. You will there see a beautiful brown smooth-handled umbrella which is not your property. Think of what the excellent prelate would have advised and bring it with you next time you come to the club.

Ever yours faithfully,

T. H. Huxley

View

Of Christopher Isherwood's *I Am a Camera* an unkind critic opined, "No Lika."

Tribute

P. G. Wodehouse's dedication of *The Heart of a Goof* has been much imitated:

To my daughter Leonora

without whose never-failing sympathy
and encouragement this book
would have been finished in half the time

Fulfillment

The editor of a monthly magazine said to G. K. Chesterton, who was very fat, "Ah, Gilbert, pregnant, I see."

"Well, at least I don't suffer from your monthly periodicals," replied Chesterton.

Flattery

Once, when James McNeill Whistler, the waspish painter, uttered a *bon mot*, Oscar Wilde remarked, "I wish I'd said that."

Whistler replied, "You will, Oscar, you will."

Wilde's reputed last words, looking at the ugly curtains in his rented bedroom: "Either they go or I do."

Jam

Henry James fancied himself an English country squire. One day the nouveau-riche owner of a neighboring estate, a mere jam manufacturer, sent back under guard one of James's employees, captured trespassing, with a haughty note.

James replied:

Dear Sir:
I am sorry my servant was caught poaching on your preserves.

Yours faithfully,

Henry James

P.S. Please forgive me for mentioning the word "preserves."

Discrimination

A dull author once complained to William Dean Howells, "I don't seem to write as well as I used to."

"Oh, yes you do . . . indeed you do," Howells reassured him; "Your *taste* is improving."

Gent

American author Michael Arlen (*The Green Hat*) as described by Rebecca West: "Every other inch a gentleman."

HIGH LIFE

Precaution

Talleyrand, captured by a bore in the Traveller's Club in London, noticed a man yawning in a far corner of the room. Clutching his interlocutor's elbow, he whispered, "Hush! you are overheard."*

Clarification

The actress Jean Harlow met Margot Asquith, whom she repeatedly addressed as "Lady Margott." Finally, Lady Margot with some asperity explained, "My dear, the 't' in my name is silent, as in *Harlow*."

---

* *In a similar fix, F. E. Smith rang for a club servant, to whom he said, "Would you mind listening to the end of this gentleman's story?"*

Conveyance

Conveyance

Alexander Woollcott was amused by Harpo Marx's battered car.

"This is my *town* car," said Harpo.

"And the town is Pompeii," replied Woollcott.

Manners

Princess Anne loves horses. At a dinner party she talked about them throughout the meal. When the coffee arrived she asked, "Could I have the sugar, please?" Her neighbor placed two lumps on his flat palm and held it out.*

Samaritan

Wilson Mizner was praising Frank Case, proprietor of the Algonquin Hotel. "A prince," declaimed Mizner, "the kind of guy who'd give you . . . my God, this *is* his shirt!"

* *See Kenneth Rose*, Kings, Queens and Courtiers.

Literary Criticism

Dorothy Parker, in a book review: "This is not a book to be tossed aside lightly. It is one to be thrown away with great force."

Diagnosis

When Justice Oliver Wendell Holmes's uncle lay on his deathbed, the nurse thrust her hand under the covers to feel his feet. "He's alive," she announced. "Nobody ever died with his feet warm."

"*John Rogers* did!*" croaked the dying man.

Definition

The longest† word in the English language is the one following the phrase, "And now, a word from our sponsor." —Hal Eaton

---

* *Burned at the stake, 1555.*

† *Among the many candidates for most beautiful word, my favorite is Maxim Gorky's:* "NOT GUILTY."

Counsel

While he was French ambassador in London, Talleyrand was called on by a poor relative, who complained of being thrown out of a gambling house; they had threatened to push him out the window if he tried to go back.

Talleyrand asked how high the windows were. On being told that they were on the fourth floor, he observed, "Since you ask my advice, I would go only to ground-floor gambling establishments. It would be even better if you knew one in a basement."

Courtesy

Edward de Vere, Earl of Oxford, offended Queen Elizabeth I by farting grossly in her presence. He retired to several years' self-imposed exile. Then he presented himself once more at court. The queen looked at him with interest and said, "My lord, We had forgot the fart!"*

* *See John Aubrey's* Brief Lives.

HISTORY

Pipeline

Disraeli, on his deathbed, was asked if he would like Queen Victoria to visit him.

"Why should I see her?" he croaked. "She'll only want me to give a message to Albert."

Fish

The old *New York Herald Tribune* once transposed the headlines of two stories in its early edition. One referred to an address by Hamilton Fish on Communist penetration of labor unions, and the other to a municipal aquarium's advice on the care of tropical fish.

Over on the rival *Daily News*, night editor George Dixon read the *Tribune*, noticed the blunder, and telephoned the *Tribune* to lodge a complaint.

Posing as an enraged Hamilton Fish, he first reached the city editor and was then referred to the managing editor himself, who apologized profusely, promising to repair the damage in later editions. Dixon/Fish slowly simmered down and finally, pretending to be mollified, hung up.

When the early morning shift of the *News* came on duty, Dixon's successor, an energetic young man named Dolan, also caught the blunder and also telephoned the *Tribune*. The city editor started to apologize all over again. Then there was a pause, and Dolan heard muttering voices. When the city editor came back on the line he sounded puzzled. "Didn't you call us just a few hours ago, Mr. Fish?" he demanded.

"Oh, no," intoned Dolan majestically. "That must have been Mr. Hamilton Fish. This is Mr. *Tropical* Fish speaking!"

Equipment

Raconteurs are fond of Gibbon's description of the Emperor Gordian: "Twenty-two acknowledged concubines, and a library of sixty-two thousand volumes, attested the variety of his inclinations, and from the productions which he left behind him, it appears that the former as well as the latter were designed for use rather than ostentation."

Of Pope John XXI's trial before the Council of Constance in 1414, Gibbon wrote, "The most scandalous charges were suppressed; the Vicar of Christ was only accused of piracy, rape, murder, sodomy and incest."

Lacuna

The Rev. Sydney Smith said of the historian Lord Macaulay, a compulsive talker, "He has occasional flashes of silence that make his conversation perfectly delightful."

Once Smith complained, "When I am dead, Macaulay, you will be sorry you never heard me speak."

Confession

The wittiest military dispatch in history was sent in 1844 by General Sir Charles Napier after his conquest of Sind (or Sindh), capital Karachi, in present-day Pakistan. It consisted of one word from the Latin liturgy: *Peccavi* ("I have sinned.").*

---

* *Although the campaign was a remarkable feat of arms (and espionage), he had indeed sinned, since as he said himself, "We have no right to seize Sind."*

Command Post

During the Civil War, Gen. John Pope liked to issue proclamations datelined, grandiosely, "Headquarters in the Saddle."

Stonewall Jackson noted wryly that the general didn't seem to distinguish his "headquarters from his hindquarters."

Update

Horace ("Go West, Young Man") Greeley insisted that "news," like "data" today, should be used in the plural. Once he cabled a reporter, ARE THERE ANY NEWS?

The reporter cabled back, NOT A NEW.

IMBROGLIOS

Spoonerisms

Warden Spooner of New College, Oxford, was famous for garbling his words. An undergraduate who had wasted the term was told he had "tasted the worm" and must leave at once by the "town drain."*

Thus the English insult: "You are the kind of man Warden Spooner would call a shining wit." A three-hundred-page collection of (dirty) French Spoonerisms, *L'Art du Contrepet*, by Jean-Jacques Pauvert, appeared in Paris in 1957. Examples: *les laborieuses populations du Cap,* or *les Anglaises qui aiment le tennis en pension.*

---

* *He had a fuzzy perception of reality, and once stopped a young man in the street to ask, "Was it you or your dear brother who was killed in the war?" G. K. Chesterton was likewise sometimes vague in practical matters. His wife once received a telegram: "Am at Crewe, where should I be?"*

Floral tribute

Floral Tribute

A man ordered an elaborate bouquet for a friend who had just opened a new office. Visiting the office, he found his wreath, with a ribbon that said "Rest in Peace."

In a rage he went back to the florist, who said, "All right, all right, so I made a mistake. But it's not *that* bad. Just think: someone in this city was buried today with a bouquet that said, 'Good Luck in Your New Location.'"

Antidote

Lady Astor once hissed at Winston Churchill, "If you were my husband, I'd put poison in your coffee."

"If I were your husband, I'd drink it," Churchill blandly replied.*

---

* *To a woman heckler who cried, "You're drunk!" he genially responded, "Ah, but tomorrow I'll be sober, and you'll still be ugly!"*

Judicious Friend

The romantic poet Gerard de Nerval strolled around Rome leading a live lobster on a leash. To puzzled observers he explained, "Because he never argues, and he knows the secrets of the deep."

Involuntary Humor

MUSIC NOTES FROM ALL OVER

[From an announcement placed in the *Bryan–College Station* (Texas) *Eagle*]

Traditional wedding music provided by Mrs. Hidlur Satre included "Yazu Joy of Mass Desire" during the prelude. The attendants march was "Trumpatune in D by Pursell." The Bride's Processional was "Bridal March For Lowengres" by Bach and the Bride's Recessional was "Toccata from Symphony Number Five" by Charles Marie Widor from the 18th Century.

—*The New Yorker*: June 1990

Broad-minded

In a BBC talk Alan Bennett made this pleasantly dotty observation: "I count myself very fortunate that as a person and as a writer I've known people of all sizes. I've known some very small people, very small people indeed.* I've also known some very tall people. And, of course, I've known quite a few more who came somewhere in between. But knowing in this way people of literally all sizes, I think my attitude is perhaps more liberal and more tolerant than someone who, whether rightly or wrongly, has confined himself to people of his own size."

---

* *Actually, small people are lucky: it rains on them later.—J.T.*

INDEX